Marcus Aurelius, Sara Carr Upton

Selections from the Thoughts of Marcus Aurelius

For Every Day in the Year

Marcus Aurelius, Sara Carr Upton

Selections from the Thoughts of Marcus Aurelius
For Every Day in the Year

ISBN/EAN: 9783337277185

Printed in Europe, USA, Canada, Australia, Japan

Cover: Foto ©Thomas Meinert / pixelio.de

More available books at **www.hansebooks.com**

SELECTIONS

FROM THE

THOUGHTS OF MARCUS AURELIUS

FOR EVERY DAY IN THE YEAR

BY

SARA CARR UPTON

NEW-YORK
PRINTED ON THE MERGENTHALER LINOTYPES

1888

Every line in this pamphlet

was set up by

THE MERGENTHALER LINOTYPE MACHINE.

THOUGHTS

OF THE

EMPEROR MARCUS AURELIUS.

JANUARY 1.

Every moment think steadily as a Roman and a man, to do what thou hast in hand with perfect and simple dignity,—in affection, in freedom and in justice.—Book II, 5.*

JANUARY 2.

How few the things are which a man need lay hold of, to be able to lead a life which flows in quiet and is like the life of the Gods.—II, 5.

JANUARY 3.

All that is from the Gods is full of Providence.—II, 3.

JANUARY 4.

Do every act of this life as if it were the last, laying aside all carelessness, aversion to the commands of reason, hypocrisy, self-love, and discontent.—II, 5.

---

* The references are to the Book and the Section of " The Thoughts of the Emperor M. Aurellus Antoninus," translated by George Long: London, George Bell & Sons, 1885, from which the selections have been taken, with very slight changes.

JANUARY 5.

Does thy soul reverence itself, or does it place its felicity in the souls of others?—II, 6.

JANUARY 6.

Do wrong to thyself. do wrong to thyself, my soul, but thou wilt have no longer the opportunity to honor thyself.—II, 6.

JANUARY 7.

Do the things external which fall upon thee, distract thee?—II, 7.

JANUARY 8.

If a man looks at death as it is in itself, and by reflecting resolves all the things which occur to the imagination into their parts, he will consider it nothing but an operation of nature.—II, 12.

JANUARY 9.

Every man's life is sufficient.—II, 6.

JANUARY 10.

Reverence for the inner spirit of a man consists in keeping it pure from passion, from thoughtlessness and from dissatisfaction with whatever comes from Gods and men.—II, 13.

JANUARY 11.

Things from men should be dear to us by reason of their kinship.—II, 13.

JANUARY 12.

Things from the gods merit veneration for their excellence.—II, 13.

JANUARY 13.

As men's ignorance of good and bad, is no less a defect than the deprivation of the power to distinguish black from white, it should move us to pity.—II, 13.

JANUARY 14.

The present is the only thing which a man can lose. for it is the only thing which he has.—II, 14.

JANUARY 15.

Though thou shouldest be going to live three thousand years, and as many times ten thousand years, still remember that no man loses any other life than that he now lives, nor lives any other life than this he now loses.—II, 14.

JANUARY 16.

The soul of a man does violence to itself when it is vexed with anything, which is itself a separation from nature. When it turns away from any man or turns toward him with anger, when it is overpowered by pleasure or pain, when it plays a part, or says or does something insincere or untrue,—when it allows any act to be without an aim and thoughtless.—II, 16.

JANUARY 17.

To keep the spirit free and pure within. one must not feel the need of another man's doing or not doing. —II, 17.

JANUARY 18.

To keep the spirit pure within, a man must do nothing without a purpose, nor yet falsely and with hypocrisy.—II, 17.

JANUARY 19.

Of human life the time is a point, and the substance is in a flux, the perception is dull. the whole body subject to putrefaction, and the soul a whirl. and fortune hard to divine, and fame a thing devoid of judgment.—II, 17.

JANUARY 20.

What is able to conduct a man? One thing and only one,—Philosophy.—II, 17.

JANUARY 21.

Keep the spirit within thee superior to pains and pleasures.—II, 17.

JANUARY 22.

Accept all that is allotted, as coming from the same source as thyself, and wait for death with a cheerful mind.—II, 17.

JANUARY 23.

If a man should have a feeling. and a deeper insight with respect to the things produced in the Universe, there is hardly one of those which follow by way of consequence which will not seem to him disposed in such a manner as to give pleasure,—the ears of corn bending down, the lion's eyebrows, the foam which flows from the mouth of wild beasts—all these are consequent on the things that are formed by nature and help to adorn them and please the mind.—III, 2.

JANUARY 24.

To die and depart from among men, if there are gods, is not a thing to be afraid of; for the gods will not involve thee in evil.—II, 11.

JANUARY 25.

Since it is possible that thou mayest depart from life this very moment, regulate every act and thought accordingly.—II, 11.

JANUARY 26.

This thou must always bear in mind—What is the nature of the whole? and what is my nature? How

Is my nature related to the nature of the whole? and what kind of a part is it of what kind of a whole?— II, 9.

JANUARY 27.

Give thyself time to learn something new and good. and cease to be whirled around.—II, 7.

JANUARY 28.

Many things will present themselves as pleasing to the man who has become truly familiar with nature and her work, which other men will miss,—he will see the real gaping jaws of wild beasts with no less pleasure than painters and sculptors feel, and he will see comeliness in an old woman and an old man.— III, 2.

JANUARY 29.

Thou hast embarked—thou hast made the voyage— thou hast come to shore—get out. If to another life, there is no want of gods there—if to a state without sensation, thou will cease to be held by pains and pleasures and to be a slave to earth and corruption. —III, 3.

JANUARY 30.

Do not waste your life in thoughts about others unless thy thoughts refer to some object of common utility.—III, 4.

JANUARY 31.

It is the part of the intellectual faculty to observe who those are whose opinions and voices give reputation.—II, 12.

FEBRUARY 1.

A man should use himself to think of those things only, about which, if one should suddenly ask, "What hast thou in thy thoughts?" he could answer with perfect openness, so that it would be plain that every-

thing in him was simple and kind, without rivalry.
envy, suspicion or anything for which he should blush.
—III, 4.

FEBRUARY 2.

A man who delays not to be among the best is like
a priest and minister of the Gods—using the deity
planted within him, which makes him uncontaminated
by pleasure, unharmed by pain, untouched by insult,
a fighter in the noblest fight, not overpowered by any
passion, deep-dyed with justice and accepting with his
soul all that happens and is his portion.—III, 4.

FEBRUARY 3.

A man should constantly think of that which is allotted to him out of the sum total of things ; and that
he must make his own acts fair and be persuaded that
his own portion is good ; for the lot assigned to each
man is both carried along with him and carries him
with it.—III, 4.

FEBRUARY 4.

A man should remember that every rational crea-
ture is his kinsman, and that to care for all men is according to man's nature.—III, 4.

FEBRUARY 5.

If a man bears in mind what kind of men those are
who do not live according to nature, and looks at
what they are at home and abroad by night and day,
and with what men they lead an impure life, he cannot
value their praise. They are not even satisfied with
themselves.—III, 4.

FEBRUARY 6.

Labor not unwillingly, nor without regard for the
common interest, nor without due consideration, nor
with distraction.—III, 5.

FEBRUARY 7.

Be cheerful and seek not eternal help, nor the tranquillity which others give.—III, 5.

FEBRUARY 8.

A man must stand erect and not be kept erect by others.—III, 5.

FEBRUARY 9.

Let not studied ornament set off thy thoughts, and be not either a man of many words nor busied about too many things.—III, 5.

FEBRUARY 10.

Let the deity within thee be the guardian of a living being, manly and of ripe age, engaged in matters political, a citizen and ruler who takes his post, like a man waiting for a signal.—III, 5.

FEBRUARY 11.

If thou findest in human life anything better than justice, truth, temperance, fortitude, turn to it, and enjoy what thou hast found to be best, only take care to make the inquiry by a sure method.—III, 6.

FEBRUARY 12.

If nothing appears better to thee than the deity planted within thee and which, as Socrates says, has detached itself from the persuasions of sense and has submitted itself to the gods and cares for mankind, if thou findest everything else smaller and of less value, then give place to nothing else.—III, 6.

FEBRUARY 13.

It is not right that such things as praise from the many, power, or enjoyment of pleasure should come into competition with what is rationally and practically good.—III, 6.

FEBRUARY 14.

He who has preferred to everything else the spirit within him and the worship of its excellence, acts no tragic part, does not groan, will not need either solitude or company and will live without either pursuing or flying from death.—III, 7.

FEBRUARY 15.

Never value anything as profitable to thyself which shall compel thee to break thy promise, to lose thy self-respect, to hate, to suspect, to curse, to act the hypocrite or do anything which needs walls and curtains.—III, 7.

FEBRUARY 16.

Simply and freely choose the better and hold to it. III, 6.

FEBRUARY 17.

A man must take care of this only all through life, that his thoughts turn not away from anything which belongs to an intelligent being and a member of a civil community. Then, if his soul is inclosed for a longer or for a shorter time in the body, he cares not at all.—III, 7.

FEBRUARY 18

Reverence the faculty which produces opinion. On this it depends whether thou shalt be ruled by opinion inconsistent with the nature of man and with the constitution of the rational being.—III, 9.

FEBRUARY 19.

The faculty which produces opinion promises freedom from hasty judgments, friendship toward men and obedience to the gods.—III, 9.

FEBRUARY 20.

Bear in mind that every man lives only this present time, which is an indivisible point, and that all the rest of his life is either past or uncertain.—III, 10.

FEBRUARY 21.

Throwing away many things, hold to these only which are few.—III, 10.

EMPEROR MARCUS AURELIUS. 11

FEBRUARY 22.

Make for thyself a definition or description of the thing presented to thee, so as to see distinctly what kind of a thing it is in its substance, in its nudity, in its complete entirety ; and tell thyself its proper name, and the names of the things of which it is compounded, and into which it will be resolved.—III, 11.

FEBRUARY 23.

Nothing is so productive of elevation of mind as to be able to examine methodically and truly every object which is presented to thee in life, and to look at each thing so as to see what it is in itself, what kind of a use it performs in the world and what value it has with reference to man.—III, 11.

FEBRUARY 24.

How long is it the nature of this thing to endure, which now makes an impression on me, and what special virtue do I need with respect to it, such as gentleness, truth, fidelity, simplicity, contentment and the rest ?—III, 11.

FEBRUARY 25.

On every occasion a man should say—" This thing comes from God—this from the spinning of the thread of destiny—and this from a kinsman of the same stock, who does not know, however, what is according to nature—but I know and for this reason must behave toward him according to the natural law of fellowship, with benevolence and justice."—III, 11.

FEBRUARY 26.

If thou workest at that which is before thee, following right reason calmly, vigorously, allowing nothing to distract thee, but keeping thy divine part pure, although bound to, give it back immediately—if thou holdest to this, expecting nothing, fearing nothing. and with heroic truth in every word and sound which thou utterest, thou wilt live happy—and there is no man able to prevent this.—III, 12.

FEBRUARY 27.

Thou wilt never do anything well which pertains to man, without having reference both to things divine and to things human.—III, 13.

FEBRUARY 28.

As physicians always have their instruments ready for cases which suddenly require their skill, so do thou have principles ready for understanding things divine and human, and for doing even the smallest things with a recollection of the bond which unites the divine and human.—III, 13.

MARCH 1.

No longer wonder at hazard.—III, 14.

MARCH 2.

It takes another kind of vision than that of the eyes merely to know how many things are signified by the words stealing, sowing, buying, keeping quiet. and seeing what ought to be done.—III, 15.

MARCH 3.

To the body befong sensations—to the soul, appetites—and to the intelligence. principles.—III, 16.

MARCH 4.

To be pulled by the strings of desire, belongs in common to wild beasts and men, and to have intelligence for what appears merely suitable. belongs to those who believe not in the gods.—III, 16.

MARCH 5.

Out of all the things common to humanity, it is peculiar to the good man to be content with the thread spun for him, and not to defile the divinity implanted in his breast; but to preserve it tranquil, not speaking contrary to truth, nor acting contrary to justice.—III, 16.

MARCH 6.

A man should come to the end of his life, pure, tranquil and ready to depart.—III. 16.

MARCH 7.

Man when ruled within according to nature makes material for himself out of that which opposes, as fire lays hold of what falls into it, consuming it and raising higher by means of this very material.—IV, 1.

MARCH 8.

Let no act be done without a purpose.—IV, 2.

MARCH 9.

Men seek retreats in the country, sea-shores and mountains—and thou too art wont to desire such things. But this is a mark of the most ordinary man, for it is in thy power, wherever thou art, to retire into thyself.—IV, 3.

MARCH 10.

Nowhere can a man retire with more quiet and freedom from trouble than within his own soul.—IV, 3.

MARCH 11.

With what art thou discontented? With the badness of men? Recall to mind that rational beings exist for one another, and that to endure is a part of justice, and that men do wrong involuntarily.—IV, 3.

MARCH 12.

Art thou dissatisfied with what is assigned thee out
of the universe? Recall to thy recollection this al-
ternative—either there is providence, or a fortuitous
concurrence of atoms.—IV, 3.

MARCH 13.

Do corporeal things fasten upon thee? Consider
that the mind mingles not with the breath, whether
the breath moves gently or violently, when the mind
has once drawn itself apart and discovered its own
power.—IV, 3.

MARCH 14.

The whole earth is a point, and how small a nook
is this thy dwelling, and what kind of people are they
who praise thee.—IV, 3.

MARCH 15.

This then remains—remember to retire into this
little territory of thy own, and above all, do not distract or strain thyself, but be free—look at things as a
man—as a human being,—as a citizen, and as a mortal.
—IV, 3.

MARCH 16.

Among the things readiest at hand turn to these
two: one is that things do not touch the soul, for they
are external and remain immovable; the other is that
all these things which thou seest, change shortly and
will no longer be.—IV, 3.

MARCH 17.

Bear in mind how many changes thou hast wit-
nessed. The universe is transformation and life is
opinion.—IV, 3.

MARCH 18.

It is natural that such things should be done by
such persons—it is a matter of necessity, and if a man

will not have it so, he will not allow the fig-tree to have juice.—IV. 6.

MARCH 19.

Take away thy opinion and there is taken away the complaint "1 am harmed." Take away the complaint "I have been harmed" and the harm has been taken away.—IV, 7.

MARCH 20.

Allow thyself a retreat into thyself, and renew thyself.—IV, 3.

MARCH 21.

That which does not make the man worse than he was, does not make his life worse, nor does it harm him without or within.—IV, 8.

MARCH 22.

If thou observest carefully thou wilt find that everything that happens, happens justly.—IV, 10.

MARCH 23.

Do not have the opinion of things which he has, who has done you wrong, nor those which he wishes you to have—but look at things as they are in truth.—IV, 11.

MARCH 24.

A man should always have these two rules in readiness—the one to do only what the ruling faculty may suggest for the use of men—the other to change his opinion if there is any one to set him right.—IV, 12.

MARCH 25.

A man's change of opinion must proceed from a persuasion of what is just or of common advantage, and not because it appears pleasant or brings reputation.—IV, 12.

MARCH 26.

Hast thou reason?—I have. Why then dost thou not use it? For if this does its own work what else dost thou wish?—IV, 13.

MARCH 27.

Thou hast existed as a part. Shalt thou disappear into that which produced thee? Say rather, thou shalt be received back into its seminal principle by transmutation.—IV, 14.

MARCH 28.

Do not act as if thou wert to live ten thousand years. Death hangs over thee. While thou livest, and it is in thy power, be good.—IV, 17.

MARCH 29.

Look not around at the depraved morals of others, but run straight along the line, and look that what thou doest, is just and pure.—IV, 18.

MARCH 30.

Everything which is in any way beautiful, is beautiful in itself, and terminates in itself, not having praise as part of itself. What thing is beautiful because it is praised, or spoiled because it is not?—IV, 20.

MARCH 31.

Is an emerald made worse if it is not praised, or gold, or ivory, or purple, or a lyre?—IV, 20.

APRIL 1.

Do not be whirled about, but in every movement have respect to justice; and on the occasion of every impression maintain the faculty of comprehension.—IV, 22.

APRIL 2.

Everything harmonizes with me which is harmonious to thee, Oh Universe. Everything is fruit to me

which thy seasons bring.   Oh Nature, from thee are
all things. in thee are all things, to thee all things
return.   The poet says, " Dear city of Cecrops"; and
wilt thou not say, " Dear city of Zeus ?"—IV, 23.

APRIL 3.

A man should take away not only unnecessary acts,
but unnecessary thoughts, so that superfluous acts will
not follow after.—IV, 24.

APRIL 4.

The greatest part of what we do and say being unnecessary, if a man takes this away, he will have more
leisure and less uneasiness.—IV, 24.

APRIL 5.
Make thyself all simplicity.—IV, 26.

APRIL 6.

Does anyone do wrong?   It is to himself he does
wrong.   Does anything happen to thee?   Out of the
Universe from the beginning, everything that happens
has been apportioned and spun out to thee.—IV, 26.

APRIL 7.

Either this is a well arranged universe or a chaos
huddled together.   But can a certain order subsist in
thee and disorder in the All?   And this too when all
things are so separated and diffused and sympathetic.
—IV, 27.

APRIL 8.

He is a runaway who flies from social reason—he is
blind who shuts the eyes of the understanding—he is
poor who has need of another, and has not from himself all things useful for life.—IV, 29.

APRIL 9.

Love the art, poor as it may be, which thou hast learned, and be content with it; and pass through the rest of life like one who has intrusted to the gods with his whole soul all that he has, making thyself neither the tyrant nor the slave of any man.—IV, 31.

APRIL 10.

It is necessary to remember that the attention given to everything has its proper value and proportion. Thus thou wilt not be dissatisfied if thou applyest thyself to smaller matters no further than is fit.—IV, 32.

APRIL 11.

What is that about which we should employ our serious pains? This one thing—thoughts just, and acts social, and words which never lie, and a disposition gladly accepting all that happens.—IV, 33.

APRIL 12.

Observe constantly that all things take place by change, and accustom thyself to consider that the nature of the universe loves nothing so much as to change the things which are, and make new things like them.—IV, 36.

APRIL 13.

Everything which exists is in a manner the seed of that which will be.—IV. 36.

APRIL 14.

Thou wilt soon die, and thou art not yet simple nor free from perturbations, nor without suspicion of being hurt by external things, nor kindly disposed to all, nor dost thou yet place wisdom only in acting justly.—IV, 37.

APRIL 15.

Examine men's ruling principles, even those of the wise—what kind of things they avoid, and what kind they pursue.—IV, 38.

APRIL 16.

Constantly regard the Universe as one living being, having one substance and one soul—and how all things are the co-operating causes of all things which exist. Observe too the continuous spinning of the thread and the contexture of the web.—IV, 40.

APRIL 17.

It is no evil for things to undergo change.—IV, 42.

APRIL 18.

Time is a river made up of the events which happen ; and is a violent stream.   As soon as a thing is seen. It is carried away and another comes in its place, and this will be carried away too.—IV, 43.

APRIL 19.

In the series of things, those which follow are always aptly fitted to those which have gone before.—IV, 45.

APRIL 20.

Things which come into existence exhibit no mere succession but a certain wonderful relationship.—IV, 45.

APRIL 21.

Pass through the little space of time of thy life conformably to nature, and end thy journey in content, just as an olive falls off when it is ripe, blessing nature who produced it and the tree on which it grew. IV, 48.

APRIL 22.

Remember on every occasion which leads thee to vexation, to apply this principle—not that this is a misfortune, but that to bear it nobly is good fortune. IV, 49.

APRIL 23.

Will what has just happened to thee prevent thee from being just. magnanimous, temperate, prudent, true—will it prevent thee from having modesty, freedom and everything by the presence of which man's nature obtains all that is his own?—IV, 49.

APRIL 24.

Unhappy am I because this has happened to me? Not so, but happy am I because I can bear it nobly. —IV, 49.

APRIL 25.

Be like the promontory against which the waves continually break: but it stands firm and tames the fury of the waters around it.—IV. 49.

APRIL 26.

In the morning when thou risest unwillingly, let this thought be present—I am rising to the work of a human being.—V, 1.

APRIL 27.

Why am I dissatisfied if I am going to do the things for which I exist. and for which I was brought into the world?—V, 1.

APRIL 28.

Have I been made to lie in the bed-clothes and keep myself warm? Dost thou not see the little plants, the little birds, the ants, spiders, bees working together to put in order their parts of the Universe —and art thou unwilling to do thy part—the work of a human being?—V, 1.

APRIL 29.

Nature has fixed bounds both to eating and drinking and sleeping, and yet thou goest beyond what is sufficient. Yet in thy acts it is not so. Thou stoppest short of what thou canst do.—V, 1.

APRIL 30.

It is easy to repel and wipe away every impression which is troublesome or unsuitable, and immediately to be in all tranquillity.—V, 2.

MAY 1.

If a thing is good to be done or said, do not consider it unworthy of thee, and be not diverted by the blame which may follow. Others have their peculiar leading principles and follow them. Thou art to follow thy own nature and the common nature—and the way of both is one.—V, 3.

MAY 2.

Thou sayest "Men cannot admire the sharpness of my wits." Be it so but there are many other qualities of which thou cannot say " I am not fitted for them by nature." Show those in thy power, sincerity, endurance, contentment, benevolence, frankness, magnanimity.—V, 5.

MAY 3.

Art thou compelled through being ill-furnished by nature, to be stingy and flatter and find fault with thy poor body, and to try to please men and to be restless in thy mind? No—by the Gods—thou mightest have been delivered from these things long ago.—V, 5.

MAY 4.

Dost thou not see how many qualities thou art immediately able to exhibit, for which thou canst not claim natural incapacity, or unfitness? Yet thou still voluntarily remainest below the mark.—V, 5.

MAY 5.

If in truth thou canst be charged with being rather slow and dull of comprehension, thou must exert thyself about this also—not neglecting it, nor yet taking pleasure in thy dulness.—V, 5.

MAY 6.

One man, when he has done a service to another. Is ready to set it down to his account as a favor conferred. Another is not ready to do this, but still, in his own mind, he thinks of the man as his debtor, and he knows what he has done. A third, in a manner, does not even know what he has done, but is like a vine which has produced grapes and seeks for nothing more, after it has once produced its proper fruit.—V, 6.

MAY 7.

A prayer of the Athenians—" Rain, rain, oh, dear Zeus, down on the ploughed fields of the Athenians and on the plains." In truth we ought to pray not at all, or in this noble and simple fashion.—V, 7.

MAY 8.

When we say things are suitable to us, we mean it as the workmen say of squared stones or walls in the pyramids. that they are suitable where they fit them to one another in some kind of connection.—V, 8.

MAY 9.

Do not be disgusted nor discouraged, nor dissatisfied, if thou dost not succeed in doing everything according to right principles.—V, 9.

MAY 10.

When thou hast failed, return back again, and be content if the greater part which thou doest is consistent with man's nature, and love this to which thou returnest.—V, 9.

MAY 11.

Remember that philosophy requires only the things which thy nature requires—but thou wouldest have something else which is not according to nature.—V, 9.

MAY 12.

He who has not one and always the same object in life cannot be one and the same all through his life.—XI, 21.

MAY 13.

About what am I now employing my own soul?—V, 11.

MAY 14.

Whose soul have I now? That of a child? of a young man? or of a feeble woman? or of a tyrant? or of a domestic animal? or of a wild beast?—V, 11.

MAY 15.

If a man should conceive certain things as being really good, such as prudence, temperance, justice. fortitude, he would not after once conceiving these, endure to listen to any other.—V, 12.

MAY 16.

No part of me will perish into non-existence, as no part of me can come into existence out of non-existence.—V, 13.

MAY 17.

Every part of me will be reduced by some change into some part of the universe, and that again will change into another part of the universe, and so on forever.—V, 13.

MAY 18.

By consequence of change, I exist, and those who begot me, and so on forever—in the other direction. —V, 13.

MAY 19.

None of those things ought to be called a man's, which do not belong to him as man. The more of such things a man deprives himself of, or the more he is deprived of any of them, and the more patiently he endures it, just in the same degree is he a better man.—V, 15.

MAY 20.

Such as are thy habitual thoughts, such also will be the character of thy mind; for the soul is dyed by the thoughts. Dye it then with a continuous series of such thoughts as these—that where a man can live, he can live well—but he must live in a palace—well then, he can live well in a palace.—V, 16.

MAY 21.

To seek what is impossible, is madness; and it is impossible that the bad should not do something of this kind.—V, 17.

MAY 22.

Nothing happens to any man which he is not formed by nature to bear.—V, 18.

MAY 23.

Something happens to a man; and either because he does not see that it has happened, or because he would show a great spirit, he remains firm and bears it well. It is a shame that ignorance and conceit should be stronger than wisdom.—V, 18.

MAY 24.

Things themselves touch not the soul, not in the

least degree—nor have they admission to the soul, nor can they turn the soul nor move the soul.—V, 19.

MAY 25.

The soul turns and moves itself alone, and whatever judgments it may think proper to make, such it makes for itself upon the things which present themselves to it.—V, 19.

MAY 26.

A man may impede my actions but he cannot impede my affects and disposition.—V, 20.

MAY 27.

Reverence that which is best in the universe—and in like manner reverence that which is best in thyself; and this is of the same kind as that.—V, 21.

MAY 28.

Consider this which is near to thee; this boundless abyss of the past and the future, in which all things disappear. How then is he not a fool who is puffed up by such things, or plagued about them, or makes himself miserable?—V, 23.

MAY 29.

Does another do me wrong? Let him look to it He has his own dispositions, his own activity. I now have what the universal nature wills me to have, and I do what my nature wills me to do.—V, 25.

MAY 30.

Live with the Gods.—V, 27.

MAY 31.

The Intelligence of the Universe is social.—V, 30.

JUNE 1.

How hast thou behaved hitherto to the gods, thy

parents, children, teachers, friends, kinsfolk, servants?
Consider that this might be said of thee: "Never has
he wronged a man in deed or word."—V, 31.

JUNE 2.

Thou canst pass thy life in an equitable flow of happiness if thou canst go the right way, and think and
act the right way.—V, 34.

JUNE 3.

If this is neither my own badness, nor the effects
of my badness; and if the common weal is not injured, why am I troubled?—V, 35.

JUNE 4.

As my earthly part is a portion given me from certain earth, and that which is water from another ele-
ment, and that which is hot and fiery from some other
source (for nothing comes out of that which is nothing,
as no existing thing returns to non-existence) so also
the intellectual part comes from some source.—IV, 4.

JUNE 5.

It is one of the acts of life, this act of dying. It
is sufficient then in this act also, to do well what we
have in hand.—VI, 2.

JUNE 6.

Look within. Let neither the peculiar quality of
anything, nor its value escape thee.—VI, 3.

JUNE 7.

The best way of avenging yourself is not to become
like that which has wronged you.—VI, 6.

JUNE 8.

Take pleasure in one thing, and rest in it, in passing
from one social act to another, thinking of God.—VI, 7.

JUNE 9.

When thou has been compelled by circumstances to be disturbed in a manner, quickly return to thyself, and do not continue out of tune longer than the compulsion lasts; for thou wilt have more mastery over the harmony by continually recurring to it.—VI. 11.

JUNE 10.

Outward show is a wonderful perverter of the reason.—VI, 13.

JUNE 11.

When thou art most sure thou art employed about things worth thy pains, it is then outward show cheats thee most.—VI, 13.

JUNE 12.

Some things are hurrying into existence and others are hurrying out of it, and of that which is coming into existence, part is already extinguished.—VI, 15.

JUNE 13.

Motions and changes are continually renewing the world, just as the uninterrupted course of time is always renewing the infinite duration of ages.—VI, 15.

JUNE 14.

In this flowing stream of life, on which there is no abiding, what is there of the things which hurry by, on which a man would set a high price?—VI, 15.

JUNE 15.

Suppose thou hast given up this worthless thing called fame, what remains that is worth valuing?   In my opinion, to develop thyself according to thy proper constitution—to which end all employments and arts lead.   For every art aims at this—that the thing which has been made, should be adapted to the work for which it has been made.—VI, 16.

JUNE 16.

A man must be in a state of perturbation who wants things ; and besides must often find fault with the gods. —VI, 16.

JUNE 17.

If thou wilt not cease to value many things, thou wilt be neither free nor sufficient for thy own happiness, nor without passion—for of necessity thou wilt be envious and jealous and suspicious of those who can take away those things, and plot against those who possess the things which are valued by thee.— VI, 16.

JUNE 18.

If a thing is difficult to be accomplished by thyself. do not think it is impossible for man—but if anything is possible for man and conformable to his nature, think that this can be obtained by thyself too.—VI, 19.

JUNE 19.

In the gymnastic exercises, suppose a man has torn thee with his nails or wounded thee. We are neither vexed nor offended, yet we are on our guard against him, not as an enemy, but we get quietly out of his way. Let thy behavior be something like this in life. Overlook many things like antagonists in a gymnasium. It is in our power to get out of the way, and to have no suspicion nor hatred.—VI, 20.

JUNE 20.

If any man is able to convince and show me that I do not think or act right, I will gladly change ; for I seek the truth by which no man was ever injured. But he who abides in error and ignorance is injured. —VI, 21.

JUNE 21.

If I do my duty, other things trouble me not. for they are either things without life, or things without reason, or things which have rambled and know not the way.—VI, 22.

JUNE 22.

On all occasions call on the Gods, and do not perplex thyself about the length of time in which thou shalt do this; for even three hours so spent are sufficient.—VI, 23.

JUNE 23.

In life remember that every duty is made up of certain parts. These it is thy duty to observe, and without being disturbed or showing anger, to go on thy way and finish that which is set before thee.— VI, 26.

JUNE 24.

Death is a cessation of the impressions through the senses, and of the pulling of the strings which move the appetites, and of the discursive movements of the thoughts, and of the service to the flesh.—VI, 28.

JUNE 25.

It is a shame for thy soul to be first to give way in this life, when the body does not give way.—VI, 29.

JUNE 26.

Keep thyself simple, good, pure, serious, free from affectation, a friend of justice, a worshipper of the gods, kind, affectionate, strenuous in all proper acts. —VI, 30.

JUNE 27.

Strive to continue to be such as philosophy wished to make thee.—VI, 30.

JUNE 28.

Reverence the gods and help men.—VI, 30.

JUNE 29.

Short is life,—there is only one fruit of this terrene life, a pious disposition and social acts.—VI, 30.

JUNE 30.

Return to thy sober senses and call thyself back;
and when thou hast roused thyself from sleep and per-
ceived they were only dreams which troubled thee,
now in thy waking state, look at the things that trouble thee as thou didst look at the dreams.—VI, 31.

JULY 1.

How many pleasures have been enjoyed by robbers,
patricides and tyrants.—VI, 34.

JULY 2.

Adapt thyself to the things with which thy lot has
been cast, and the men among whom thou hast received thy portion. Love them, but love them truly.
—VI, 39.

JULY 3.

We are all working together for one end. Some
with knowledge and design, and others without know-
ing what they do—as men who sleep.—VI, 42.

JULY 4.

Does the sun undertake to do the work of the rain,
or Æsculapius the work of Earth, the Fruit-Bearer?
And how is it with respect to each of the stars? Are
they not different, and yet work together to the same
end?—VI, 43.

JULY 5.

Whatever is profitable to any man, is profitable to
other men.- VI, 45.

JULY 6.

Whatever happens to any man this is for the interest of the universal.—VI, 45.

JULY 7.

One thing here is worth a great deal—to pass thy

life in truth and justice, with a benevolent disposition even to liars and unjust men.—VI, 47.

JULY 8.

When thou wishest to delight thyself. think of the virtues of those who live with thee.   For instance. the activity of one. the modesty of another. the liberality of a third.—VI, 48.

JULY 9.

Accustom thyself to attend carefully to what is said by another, and as much as possible bo in the speaker's mind.—VI, 53.

JULY 10.

That which is not good for the swarm, neither is it good for the bee.—VI, 54.

JULY 11.

How many, together with whom I came into the world, have already gone out of it.—VI. 56.

JULY 12.

No man will hinder thee from living according to the reason of thy own nature—nothing will happen to thee contrary to the reason of the universal nature.—VI, 58.

JULY 13.

To the jaundiced, honey tastes bitter; to those bitten by mad dogs water causes fear.   Why then am I angry?   Has a false opinion less power than bile in the jaundiced. or the poison of a mad dog?—VI, 57.

JULY 14.

What kind of people are those whom men wish to please, and for what objects, and by what kind of acts?—VI, 59.

JULY 15.

Let it make no difference to thee whether thou art cold or warm, sleepy or wakeful, ill-spoken of. or praised, if thou art doing thy duty.—VI, 2.

JULY 16.

I can have that opinion about anything which I ought to have.—VII, 2.

JULY 17.

The things which. are external to my mind, have no relation at all to my mind. Let this be the state of thy affects, and thou standest erect.—VII, 2.

JULY 18.

The idle business of show, plays on the stage, flocks of sheep, herds, a bone cast to little dogs. a bit of bread into fish-ponds, laborings of ants and burden carrying, runnings about of frightened little mice, puppets pulled by strings,—all alike—it is thy duty in the midst of such things to show good humor and not a proud air.—VII, 3.

JULY 19.

Every man is worth just so much as the things about which he busies himself.—VII, 3.

JULY 20.

In discourse thou must attend to what is said. and in every movement thou must observe what is doing. And in the one, thou shouldest see immediately to what end it refers, and in the other watch carefully what is the thing signified.—VII, 4.

JULY 21.

Is my understanding sufficient for this work or not? If it is sufficient. I use it for the work as an instrument given by the universal nature.—VII. 5.

JULY 22.

If my understanding is not sufficient for this work, I retire from it and give way to him who is able to do it better; unless there be some reason why I ought not to retire, when I do it as well as I can, taking to help me the man who can be most useful for the general good.—VII, 5.

JULY 23.

Whatsoever I can do by myself, or with another, ought to be directed to this only; to that which is useful and well suited to society.—VII, 5.

JULY 24.

Be not ashamed to be helped, for it is thy business to do thy duty like a soldier in the assault on a town. If thou are lame and canst not mount the battlements, with the help of another it is possible.—VII, 7.

JULY 25.

Let not future things disturb thee, for thou wilt come to them if it shall be necessary, having with thee the same reason which thou now usest for present things.—VII, 8.

JULY 26.

All things are implicated with one another, and the bond is holy.—VII, 9.

JULY 27.

To the rational being, the act which is according to nature is according to reason.—VII, 11.

JULY 28.

Be thou erect, or be made erect.—VII, 12.

JULY 29.

Often say to thyself "I am a member of a system of rational beings"; if thou feelest thyself separated

thou dost not yet love men from thy heart. Good
delights thee not for its own sake, and as doing good
to thyself, but as a thing of propriety.—VII, 13.

JULY 30.

Unless I think that what has happened is an evil
I am not injured; and it is in my power not to think
so.—VII, 14.

JULY 31.

Whatever any one does or says, I must be good,
just as if the gold or the emerald or the purple were
always saying this, " Whatever any one does or says,
I must be emerald and keep my color."—VII, 15.

AUGUST 1.

Is any man afraid of change? Why. what that is
useful, can be accomplished without change? Canst
thou take a bath unless the wood undergoes a change?
Canst thou be nourished unless the food undergoes a
change? Dost thou then not see that for thyself also
to change is just the same and is frequently necessary
for the universal nature?—VII, 18.

AUGUST 2.

Near is thy forgetfulness of all things; and near the
forgetfulness of thee by all things.—VII, 21.

AUGUST 3.

It is peculiar to man to love even those who do
wrong. And this happens, if when they do wrong, it
occurs to thee they are kinsmen, and that they do
wrong through ignorance and unintentionally and that
soon both of you will die—and above all, that the
wrong-doer has done thee no harm for he has not
made thy ruling faculty worse than it was before.—
VII, 22.

AUGUST 4.

A scowling look is altogether unnatural, and when often worn, the result is that all comeliness dies away, —and at last is so completely extinguished, that it cannot be lighted up at all.—VII, 24.

AUGUST 5.

When a man has done thee any wrong, immediately think with what opinion about good or evil he has done wrong; for when thou hast seen this, thou wilt pity him and neither wonder nor be angry.—VII, 26.

AUGUST 6.

Think not so much of what thou hast not, as of what thou hast.—VII, 27.

AUGUST 7.

Retire into thyself. Do what is just and thus secure tranquillity.—VII, 28.

AUGUST 8.

Confine thyself to the present.—VII, 29.

AUGUST 9.

Understand well what happens to thee or to another.—VII, 29.

AUGUST 10.

Think of thy last hour.—VII, 29.

AUGUST 11.

Let the wrong which was done by a man stay where the wrong was done.—VII, 29.

AUGUST 12.

Direct thy attention to what is said.—VII, 30.

AUGUST 13.

Let thy understanding enter into the things that are doing, and into the things that do them.—VII, 30.

AUGUST 14.

Adorn thyself with simplicity and modesty and with indifference to the things which lie between virtue and vice.—VII, 31.

AUGUST 15.

Love mankind; follow God.—VII, 31.

AUGUST 16.

The pain which is intolerable carries us off, but that which lasts a long time is tolerable.—VII, 33.

AUGUST 17.

From Antisthenes.—It is royal to do good and to be abused.—VII, 36.

AUGUST 18.

It is a base thing for the countenance to be obedient and to regulate and compose itself as the mind commands, and for the mind not to be regulated and composed by itself—VII, 37.

AUGUST 19.

It is not right to vex ourselves at things, for they care naught about it.—Euripides.—VII. 38.

AUGUST 20.

Life must be reaped like the ripe ears of corn. One man is born; another dies.—Euripides.—VII, 40.

AUGUST 21.

If tne gods care not for me and for my children, there is a reason for it.—VII, 41.

AUGUST 22.

From Plato.—A man who is good for anything at
all, ought not to compute the hazard of life or death,
but should rather look to this in all he does—is it just
or unjust?—VII, 44.

AUGUST 23.

Wherever a man has placed himself thinking it the
best place for him, or has been placed by a command-
er, there he ought to stay and abide the hazard, taking nothing into account—neither death or everything
else—before the baseness of deserting his post.—VII,
45.

‘ AUGUST 24.

Look around at the courses of the stars as if thou
wert going along with them—and constantly consider
the changes of the elements into one another—for such
thoughts purge away the filth of the terrene life.—
VII, 47.

AUGUST 25.

That which has grown from the earth, to the earth;
that which has sprung from heavenly seed, back to
the heavenly realms returns.—Euripides.—VII. 50.

AUGUST 26.

Love that only which happens to thee and is spun
with the thread of thy destiny.   For what is more
suitable?—VII, 57.

AUGUST 27.

Another may be more expert in throwing his op-
ponent, but let him not be more social nor more modest, nor better disciplined to meet all that happens,
nor more considerate with respect to the faults of his
neighbors.—VII, 52.

AUGUST 28.

Where my work can be done conformably to the

reason which is common to gods and men, there we
have nothing to fear.—VII, 53.

AUGUST 29.

Consider thyself to be dead and to have completed
thy life up to the present time, and live according to
nature the remainer that is allowed thee.—VII, 56.

AUGUST 30.

Why art thou not altogether intent upon the right
way of making use of the things which happen to thee,
for then thou wilt use them well, and they will be
material to work on.—VII, 58.

AUGUST 31.

Attend to thyself and resolve to be a good man in
every act which thou doest.—VII, 58.

SEPTEMBER 1.

Look within. Within is the fountain of good, and
it will ever bubble up if thou wilt ever dig.—VII, 59.

SEPTEMBER 2.

The art of life is like the wrestler's art, that it
should stand firm and ready to meet onsets which are
sudden and unexpected.—VII. 61.

SEPTEMBER 3.

Constantly observe those whose approbation thou
wishest, and see what is their ruling principle. For
then thou wilt neither blame those who offend involuntarily, nor wilt thou want their approbation if thou
lookest at the sources of their opinions and appetites.
—VII, 62.

SEPTEMBER 4.

Epicurus says that pain is neither intolerable nor
everlasting if thou bearest in mind that it has its

limits, and if thou addest nothing to it in imagination.—VII, 64.

SEPTEMBER 5.

Take care not to feel towards the inhuman as they feel towards men.—VII, 65.

SEPTEMBER 6.

Be not idly vexed at man's villany, neither make yourself a slave to any man's ignorance.—VII, 66.

SEPTEMBER 7.

It is very possible to be a divine man and to be recognized as such by no one.—VII, 67.

SEPTEMBER 8.

Very little is needed for a happy life. Because thou hast despaired of becoming a dialectician and skilled in the knowledge of nature, do not for this reason renounce the hope of being both free and modest and social and obedient to God.—VII, 67.

SEPTEMBER 9.

The use shall say to that which falls under the hand "Thou art the thing I was seeking"; for to me that which presents itself to me is always material for virtue, and for the exercise of art which belongs to man or to God.—VII, 68.

SEPTEMBER 10.

The perfection of moral character consists in this —in passing each day as thy last, in being neither excited nor torpid. nor playing the hypocrite.—VII, 69.

SEPTEMBER 11.

It is a ridiculous thing for a man not to fly from his own badness which is possible; but it is impossible to fly from that of other men.—VII, 71.

SEPTEMBER 12.

When thou hast done a good act and another has received it, why dost thou look for more, as fools do. either to have the reputation of having done a good act, or to obtain a return?—VII, 73.

SEPTEMBER 13.

Throw away the thought how thou shalt seem to others ; and be content to live as thy nature wills— in the belief that there is nothing good for man that does not make him just, temperate, manly, free—and there is nothing bad that does not do to the contrary. —VIII, 1.

SEPTEMBER 14.

On the occasion of every act, ask " How is this in respect of me?" " Shall I repent of it?"—VIII, 2.

SEPTEMBER 15.

Is what I am doing the work of an intelligent, living, social being and of one who is under the same law with God?—VIII, 2.

SEPTEMBER 16.

Consider that men will do the same things nevertheless, even though thou shouldest burst.—VIII, 4.

SEPTEMBER 17.

This is the chief thing.   Be not perturbed, for all things are according to the nature of the universal. —VIII, 5.

SEPTEMBER 18.

It is thy duty to be a good man, and what man's nature demands, do that without turning aside.—VIII, 5.

SEPTEMBER 19.

Speak as it seems to thee most just, only let it be with a good disposition, with modesty and without hypocrisy.—VIII, 5.

SEPTEMBER 20.

The nature of the universal is change. Yet we need not fear anything new.—VIII, 6.

SEPTEMBER 21.

Every particular nature is part of a common nature, as the leaf is part of the common nature of the plant. —VIII, 7.

SEPTEMBER 22.

Examine not to discover that any one thing compared with any other single thing is equal in all respects, but compare all the parts taken together of one thing with all the parts' taken together of another.—VIII, 7.

SEPTEMBER 23.

Thou hast not leisure (or ability) to read. But thou hast leisure (or ability) to check thy arrogance—to be superior to pleasure or pain, or to the love of fame—and leisure not to be vexed at stupid or ungrateful people, nay even to care for them.—VIII, 8.

SEPTEMBER 24.

Let no man any more hear thee finding fault with life or with thy own life.—VIII, 9.

SEPTEMBER 25.

This thing, what is it in itself, in its own constitution, its substance. Its material, its casual nature—and what is it doing in the world? And how long ' does it subsist?—VIII, 11.

SEPTEMBER 26.

Whatever man thou meetest, say to thyself, what opinions has he about good and bad? For if he has such and such opinions with respect to pleasure and pain and their causes—with respect to fame and ignominy, death and life—it is not strange that he does such and such things—and I shall bear in mind that he is compelled to.—VIII, 14.

SEPTEMBER 27.

Remember that as it is a shame to be surprised. If the fig tree produces figs, so it is a shame to be surprised that the world produces the things of which it is productive.—VIII, 15.

SEPTEMBER 28.

Remember that to change thy opinion and to follow him who corrects thy error, is as consistent with freedom as to persist in thy error.—VIII, 16.

SEPTEMBER 29.

If it is a thing in thy own power, why dost thou do it? If it is in the power of another, whom dost thou blame?—VIII, 17.

SEPTEMBER 30.

That which has died, falls not out of the universe. —VIII, 18.

OCTOBER 1.

Everything exists for some end—a horse, a vine. For what purpose art thou? To enjoy pleasure? See if common sense allows this.—VIII, 19.

OCTOBER 2.

Short lived are both the praiser and the praised— and all this is a nook in this part of the world—and not even here do all agree, not even any one with himself.—VIII, 21.

OCTOBER 3.

Attend to the matter which is before thee; whether it is an opinion, an act, or a word.—VIII, 22.

OCTOBER 4.

Thou sufferest this justly, for thou choosest this rather to become good to-morrow than to-day.—VIII, 22.

OCTOBER 5.

Man has three relations—one to the body which surrounds him, one to the divine cause from which all things come to all, and one to those who live with him.—VIII, 27.

OCTOBER 6.

Pain is either an evil to the body—then let the body say what it thinks about it—or to the soul. But the soul can maintain its serenity and not think it an evil. Every judgment, desire or aversion is within, and no evil ascends so high.—VIII, 28.

OCTOBER 7.

Speak both in the senate and to every man appropriately without any affectation. Use plain discourse.—VIII, 30.

OCTOBER 8.

It is thy duty to order thy life well in every single act.—VIII, 32.

OCTOBER 9.

Receive prosperity without arrogance, and be ready to let it go.—VIII, 33.

OCTOBER 10.

Didst thou ever see a hand cut off, or a foot or a head lying anywhere apart from the rest of the body? Such does a man make himself who is not content with what happens, and who separates himself from others and does anything unsocial.—VIII, 34.

OCTOBER 11.

Do not disturb thyself by thinking of the whole of thy life.—VIII, 36.

OCTOBER 12.

Let not thy thoughts at once embrace all the various troubles thou mayest expect, but on every occasion ask thyself. "What is there in this, past bearing?"
—VIII, 36.

OCTOBER 13.

If thou takest away thy opinion about that which appears to give thee pain. thou thyself standest in perfect security.—VIII, 40.

OCTOBER 14.

Different things delight different men, but I delight to look at and receive all with welcome eyes and to use everything according to its value.—VIII, 43.

OCTOBER 15.

Take me and cast me where thou wilt. for there I shall keep my divine part tranquil if it can feel and act conformably to its proper constitution.--VIII, 45.

OCTOBER 16.

Is change of place sufficient reason why my soul should be unhappy, and worse than it was—depressed, expanded, shrinking, affrighted?—VIII, 45.

OCTOBER 17.

The mind which is free from passions is a citadel
—VIII, 48.

OCTOBER 18.

A cucumber is bitter—Throw it away—There are briars in the road—turn aside from them—This is enough.—VIII, 50.

OCTOBER 19.

Be not sluggish in thy actions, nor without method in thy conversation, nor wandering in thy thoughts—nor let there be inward contention in thy soul. nor external effusion.—VIII, 51.

OCTOBER 20.

In life be not so busy as to have no leisure.—VIII, 51.

OCTOBER 21.

If a man should stand by a limpid pure spring and curse it, still the spring never ceases sending up good water.—VIII, 51.

OCTOBER 22.

Dost thou wish to be praised by a man who curses himself thrice every hour? Wouldst thou wish to please a man who does not please himself?—VIII, 53.

OCTOBER 23.

Generally, wickedness does no harm at all to the Universe, and particularly one man's wickedness does no harm to another. It is only harmful to him who has it in his power to be released from it as soon as he shall choose.—VIII. 55.

OCTOBER 24.

Men exist for one another. Teach them then, or bear with them.—VIII. 59.

OCTOBER 25.

Enter into every man's ruling faculty—and also let every other man enter into thine.—VIII. 61.

OCTOBER 26.

He who pursues pleasure will not abstain from injustice.—IX, 1.

OCTOBER 27.

Has not experience induced thee yet to fly from the pestilence, and hast thou determined to abide with vice?—IX, 2.

OCTOBER 28.

Do not despise death, but be well content with it,

since it is one of those things which nature wills.—
IX, 3.

OCTOBER 29.

He who does wrong, does wrong against himself.
—IX, 4.

OCTOBER 30.

He who acts unjustly is unjust to himself—because
he makes himself bad.—IX, 4.

OCTOBER 31.

Not only he who does a certain thing acts unjustly,
but often he who does not do a certain thing.—IX, 5.

NOVEMBER 1.

If thou art able, correct by teaching those who do
wrong. If thou canst not, remember that indulgence
is given thee for this purpose.—IX, 11.

NOVEMBER 2.

Labor not as one who is wretched, nor yet as one
who would be pitied or admired.—IX, 12.

NOVEMBER 3.

To-day I have got out of all trouble, or rather I
have cast out all trouble, for it was not outside, but
within and in my opinions.—IX, 13.

NOVEMBER 4.

All things are changing. Thou thyself art in continuous mutation and destruction, and so is the universe.—IX, 19.

NOVEMBER 5.

It is thy duty to leave another man's wrongful act,
there where it is.—IX, 20.

NOVEMBER 6.

Turn thy thoughts to thy life as a child, as a youth,

as a man, and as an old man—for in these also every
change was a death.   Is this anything to fear?—IX,
21.

NOVEMBER 7.

Examine thy own ruling faculty that thou mayest
make it just.—IX, 22.

NOVEMBER 8.

Examine the ruling faculty of the Universe, that
thou mayest remember of what thou art a part.—IX.
22.

NOVEMBER 9.   ·

Examine the ruling faculty of thy neighbor, that
thou mayest know if he has acted ignorantly or with
knowledge, and that thou mayest consider that he is
akin to thee.—IX, 22.

NOVEMBER 10.

As thou thyself art a component part of a social
system, so let every act of thine be a component part
of social life.—IX. 23.

NOVEMBER 11.

Whatever act of thine has no reference either immediately or remotely to a social end, tears asunder
thy life, does not allow it to be one, and is in the
nature of a mutiny.—IX, 23.

NOVEMBER 12.

Quarrels of little children and their sports, and
poor spirits carrying about dead bodies—such is everything.—IX, 24.

NOVEMBER 13.

Thou hast endured infinite troubles, through not
being contented with thy ruling faculty when it does
the things which it is constituted by nature to do.
—IX, 26.

NOVEMBER 14.

When another blames thee or hates thee, or when men say injurious things about thee, approach their poor souls, penetrate within and see what kind of men they are. Thou wilt find thou hast no reason to be troubled. Thou must be well disposed to them. however, for by nature they are friends.—IX. 26.

NOVEMBER 15.

If a man reflects on the changes and transformations which follow one another like wave after wave, and on their rapidity, he will despise everything perishable.—IX, 28.

NOVEMBER 16.

The universal cause is like a winter torrent.—It carries everything along with it.—IX, 29.

NOVEMBER 17.

Simple and modest is the work of philosophy. Draw me not aside to insolence and pride.—IX, 29.

NOVEMBER 18.

Thou canst remove out of the way many useless things among those which disturb thee, for they lie entirely in thy opinion.—IX, 32.

NOVEMBER 19.

When men think they do harm by their blame or good by their praise,—what an idea!—IX, 34.

NOVEMBER 20.

Loss is nothing else than change.—IX, 35.

NOVEMBER 21.

Enough of this wretched life and murmuring and apish tricks.—IX, 37.

NOVEMBER 22.

Why art thou disturbed? What is there new in this? What unsettles thee? Is it the form of the thing? Look at it—Is it the matter? Look at it—Besides these there is nothing.—IX, 37.

NOVEMBER 23.

If any man has done wrong the harm is his own. But perhaps he has not done wrong.—IX, 38.

NOVEMBER 24.

When thou blamest a man as faithless or ungrateful, turn to thyself. For the fault is manifestly thy own, whether thou didst trust that a man who had such a disposition would keep his promise, or when conferring thy kindness thou didst not do it absolutely and in such a way as to have received all the profit from thy very act.—IX, 42.

NOVEMBER 25.

Wilt thou then, my soul, never be good, and simple, and one, and naked,—more manifest than the body which surrounds thee.—X, 1.

NOVEMBER 26.

Remember that thou art formed by nature to bear everything which depends on thy own opinion to make bearable, by thinking it either for thy interest, or for thy duty to do this.—X, 3.

NOVEMBER 27.

If a man is mistaken, instruct him kindly and show him his error. But if thou art not able, blame thyself—or blame not even thyself.—X, 4.

NOVEMBER 28.

When thou hast assumed these names, good, true, modest, rational, a man of equanimity and magnanimous, take care thou dost not change them, and if thou shouldest lose them, quickly return to them.— X, 8.

NOVEMBER 29.

It will greatly help thee to keep the names which thou hast assumed of good, true, modest, rational, if thou wilt remember the gods—that they do not wish to be flattered, but wish all reasonable beings to be made like themselves.—X, 8.

NOVEMBER 30.

Equanimity is voluntary acceptance of the things assigned to thee by the common nature.—X, 8.

DECEMBER 1.

Magnanimity is the elevation of the intelligent part above the pleasures or pains of the flesh, above fame, death and all such things.—X, 8.

DECEMBER 2.

It will help thee if thou rememberest that what does the work of a fig tree is a fig tree, that what does the work of a bee is a bee, and that what does the work of a man is a man.—X, 8.

DECEMBER 3.

A spider is proud when it has caught a fly, a man when he has caught a poor hare, or taken a little fish in a net—Are these not robbers, if thou lookest at their opinions?—X, 10.

DECEMBER 4.

Acquire the contemplative way of seeing how all things change into one another. Nothing is so much adapted to produce magnanimity.—X, 11.

DECEMBER 5.

If thou seest clear, go by this way content without turning back. If thou dost not see clear, stop and take the best advisers. But if any other things oppose thee, go on according to thy powers with due consideration, keeping to that which appears to be just.—X, 12.

DECEMBER 6.

If thou dost fail, let it be in attempting what is just.—X, 12.

DECEMBER 7.

Inquire of thyself as soon as thou wakest from sleep, whether it will make any difference to thee, if another does what is just and right. It will make no difference.—X, 13.

DECEMBER 8.

Short is the little which remains to thee of life— Live as on a mountain.—X, 15.

DECEMBER 9.

No longer talk at all about the kind of man that a good man ought to be; but be such.—X, 16.

DECEMBER 10.

When thou art offended at any man's fault, forthwith turn to thyself and reflect in what like manner thou dost err—for example, in thinking that money is a good thing, or pleasure, or a bit of reputation, and the like.—X, 30.

DECEMBER 11.

All things that happen in thy life are exercises for the reason. Persevere, therefore, and make all things thy own, as the blazing fire makes flame and brightness of all that is thrown into it.—X, 31.

DECEMBER 12.

Let it not be in any man's power to say truly of thee that thou art not simple, or that thou art not good—This is in thy power.—X, 32.

DECEMBER 13.

Accustom thyself as much as possible to inquire—for what object does this man do this. But begin with thyself and examine thyself first.—X, 37.

DECEMBER 14.

Have I done something for the general interest? Well, then I have had my reward.—XI, 4.

DECEMBER 15.

A branch cut off from the adjacent branch must of necessity be cut off from the whole tree also—So too a man, when he is separated from another man, has fallen off from the whole social community.—XI, 8.

DECEMBER 16.

Look to guard steady judgment and action, as well as gentleness, to those who would hinder and trouble thee.—XI, 9.

DECEMBER 17.

Suppose any man shall despise me. Let him look to it. But I will look to this, that I neither do nor say anything deserving of contempt. Shall any man hate me? Let him look to it. But I will be mild and benevolent, noble and honest.—X, 13.

DECEMBER 18.

Men despise one another, and flatter one another; and men wish to raise themselves above one another, and do crouch before one another.—XI, 14.

DECEMBER 19.

The man who is honest and good, ought to be like

the man who smells strong, so that the bystander, when he comes near, must smell him whether he chooses or not.—XI, 15.

DECEMBER 20.

A man must learn a great deal to enable him to pass a correct judgment on another man's acts.—XI. 18.

DECEMBER 21.

A good disposition is invincible if it is genuine; and not an affected smile and acting a part.—XI, 18.

DECEMBER 22.

In the same degree that a man's mind is free from passion, in the same degree it is nearer to strength.—XI, 18.

DECEMBER 23.

As a sense of pain is characteristic of weakness, so also is anger. He who yields to pain and he who yields to anger, both are wounded and both are subdued.—XI, 18.

DECEMBER 24.

Socrates used to call the opinions of the many Lamiae—bugbears to frighten children.—XI, 23.

DECEMBER 25.

Epictetus says "the unripe grape, the ripe bunch, the dried grape are all changes—not into nothing, but into something which exists not yet."—XI, 35.

DECEMBER 26.

Epictetus says "No man can rob us of our free-will."—XI, 36.

DECEMBER 27.

If it is not right, do not do it.   If it is not true, do not say it.—XII, 17.

DECEMBER 28.

Practise thyself in the things thou despairest of accomplishing; for even the left hand holds the bridle stronger than the right, because in that it has been practised.—XII, 6.

DECEMBER 29.

I have often wondered how it is that each man loves himself better than all the rest of men, but yet sets less value on his own opinion of himself, than on the opinion of others.—XII, 4.

DECEMBER 30.

What is there now in my mind? Is it fear or suspicion, or desire, or any such thing? Then perceive that thou hast in thee something better and diviner than the things which cause those various effects and pull thee by their strings.—XII, 19.

DECEMBER 31.

When thou art troubled, thou hast forgotten that all things happen according to the universal nature—forgotten that another man's wrong act is nothing to thee—forgotten that the kinship between man and the race is not of blood or seed, but of intelligence—forgotten that every man's intelligence is an efflux from the Deity and that nothing is a man's own—but even his child and his own body and his very soul came from the Deity—and thou hast forgotten that every man lives the present time only and loses only this.—XII, 26.

www.ingramcontent.com/pod-product-compliance
Lightning Source LLC
Chambersburg PA
CBHW031802090426
42739CB00008B/1132